A CENTURY
OF STORIES
NEW HANOVER COUNTY PUBLIC LIBRARY
1906-2006

Children's Authors

Barbara Park

Jill C. Wheeler
ABDO Publishing Company

visit us at
www.abdopublishing.com

Published by ABDO Publishing Company, 4940 Viking Drive, Edina, Minnesota 55435.
Copyright © 2007 by Abdo Consulting Group, Inc. International copyrights reserved in all
countries. No part of this book may be reproduced in any form without written permission from
the publisher. The Checkerboard Library™ is a trademark and logo of ABDO Publishing
Company.

Printed in the United States.

Cover Photo: Random House
Interior Photos: Corbis pp. 9, 10, 11, 17; Getty Images p. 7; Random House pp. 5, 15, 19, 21, 23;
    Wenn Images p. 13

Series Coordinator: Megan Murphy
Editors: Rochelle Baltzer, Megan Murphy
Art Direction: Neil Klinepier

Library of Congress Cataloging-in-Publication Data

Wheeler, Jill C., 1964-
    Barbara Park / Jill C. Wheeler.
        p. cm. -- (Children's authors)
    Includes index.
    ISBN-10 1-59679-766-5
    ISBN-13 978-1-59679-766-6
    1. Park, Barbara--Juvenile literature. 2. Authors, American--20th century--Biography--
Juvenile literature. 3. Children's stories--Authorship--Juvenile literature. I. Title. II. Series.

    PS3566.A6725Z95 2006
    813'.54--dc22
                                                                            2005023999

Contents

One Funny Writer

She always has something to say. She sometimes says it wrong. She often gets in trouble. And she's only in the first grade. Meet Junie B. Jones.

Junie B. is the creation of children's book author Barbara Park. Park has been called one of the funniest writers around. She has won more than 40 awards for her work, including 25 **Children's Choice Awards**. Children of all ages are able to identify with her believable, likable characters. Park's **unique** style makes both kids and parents laugh.

Park says she wants to challenge her readers, but she doesn't want to overwhelm them. Her books are not intended to teach children lessons. She may write about an important issue, yet she tells the story with humor and sensitivity.

Since 1992, Park has written more than 20 Junie B. Jones titles. The series has sold about 25 million copies in North America alone. Readers in Spain, Italy, and Indonesia also have Junie B. Jones books in their languages. Park has written 13 other novels for children, too.

Park never planned to be a writer. She used to think writing was as enjoyable as eating brussels sprouts. But today, her readers are glad she learned to like her vegetables!

Before she married, Park's initials were BLT, like the sandwich!

Grade School Comedian

Barbara Lynne Tidswell was born on April 21, 1947, in Mount Holly, New Jersey. Her father, Brooke, was a banker and a business owner. He also served on the school board for a time. Barbara's mother, Doris, was a secretary. Barbara has one brother, Brooke, who is two years older than she is.

Barbara remembers Mount Holly as a great place to grow up. Her family often went to Long Beach Island in the summer. Barbara loved reading comic books and playing hide-and-seek with her brother. She liked to hide in the clothes hamper. Unfortunately, that was the first place her brother usually looked.

Barbara may not have enjoyed writing yet, but she did enjoy going to school. And she loved to talk! Barbara was always chatting in class. When she thought of something funny to say, she usually said it out loud. Her teachers did not always like that, however. They never thought her comments were as funny as Barbara thought they were.

In the first grade, Barbara had to visit the principal because of her chattiness. Her first grade report card also made note of her behavior. It said the teachers were trying to teach Barbara not to talk when others were talking.

As a child, Barbara's main goal was to perform on the popular television show **The Mickey Mouse Club.** *She said she never thought about the fact that she could not sing or dance like the kids on the show. However, she did seem to have a talent for making people laugh.*

Halfhearted Teacher

Barbara enjoyed high school, too. She attended Rancocas Valley Regional High School in Mount Holly. Before this time, Barbara had not been much of a reader. But, she remembers reading a special book in her second year of high school. It was called *The Catcher in the Rye*. In this book, the **narrator** tells the story directly to the reader.

Barbara loved *The Catcher in the Rye*. She realized that a fictional character could seem as real as an actual person. The experience hooked Barbara on to reading.

In 1965, Barbara began college at Rider University in New Jersey. She studied to become a high school history and political science teacher. She did not really want to be a teacher. But, she thought she could make history and politics more fun for students.

Barbara spent two years at Rider. Then she transferred to the University of Alabama. During this time, she met Richard Park. Richard was in the air force. The two married in summer 1969 after Barbara graduated from college.

Barbara met her husband while she was in college and he was in the air force.
The air force is the branch of the military that specializes in air warfare.
Some members of the air force fly fighter planes such as this F-16 Falcon.

A New Career

However, Park was still unsure about what she wanted as a career. She realized that she didn't want to teach. Soon, she and Richard started a family. Barbara wanted something she could do while she was home with her sons, Steven and David.

Park found the perfect solution in her late 20s. She began writing. The first thing Park ever had published was a Hallmark greeting card. She received $50 for it. At first, she thought she had found a new career. Yet she never sold another card.

Next, Park tried writing for grown-ups. She sent a story to a newspaper magazine. Unfortunately, the editors changed a lot of her story. It was not as funny anymore. So, Park continued her search for the right **audience**.

As a child, Park liked to read comic books. Her favorite comics series were Archie and Richie Rich. Park says it was her love of reading that made her try writing.

Park's only job for Hallmark was composing a mean-spirited birthday card. She wrote the verse inside, and an artist like this one designed the cover art.

Two Years to Write

Park's life took a new turn in 1978. By then, Richard had left the air force. The family had moved to Arizona, where Richard now worked in **real estate**.

One day, one of Park's sons brought home a book from school. The book was Judy Blume's *Tales of a Fourth Grade Nothing*. Park read it and realized Blume's style of humor was similar to her own. Park began to wonder if she might be a good writer for the children's fiction **genre**, too.

Park set a goal for herself. She would **dedicate** two years to writing. Within that time, she would work her hardest to write and publish a novel for young readers.

Park recalls that she was lucky to be able to set that goal. First, her boys were both in school. That gave her plenty of time during the day to write. Also, her husband earned enough money for the family to live on. Park realized many would-be writers would give anything to be in her shoes. She knew she should take advantage of the situation.

Park began to think of book ideas. She wanted to create believable stories about real-life situations. Readers needed to be able to identify with her characters. Most of all, the stories had to be funny. She wanted her readers to enjoy themselves.

Judy Blume's book **Tales of a Fourth Grade Nothing** *was Park's inspiration to write a children's book of her own!*

Getting Published

By 1981, Park had written three novels for young people. The first is about an older brother who tries to dump off his younger brother on some elderly neighbors. She called it *Operation: Dump the Chump*.

Her second book is titled *Skinnybones*. It is about a young boy who is the smallest player in his baseball league. Life seems pretty unfair. Then he wins a contest to be in a television commercial. Suddenly everything changes.

Park's third book is called *Don't Make Me Smile*. It is the story of a boy named Charlie. The book deals with how Charlie handles the divorce of his parents.

Park was very excited when she sent *Operation: Dump the Chump* to a publisher. However, the **manuscript** was rejected three times before the publishing company Alfred A. Knopf agreed to publish it. Knopf's editors liked the book so much they asked if she had written anything else.

Park quickly sent Knopf the other two books. *Don't Make Me Smile* was published first, in 1981. *Operation: Dump the Chump* and *Skinnybones* followed in 1982.

Park later wrote follow-ups to both Don't Make Me Smile and Skinnybones.

From Silly to Serious

Soon, Park's two-year goal turned into a career. Originally, she wrote about boys because she had sons. But eventually, she realized girl characters could be just as fun.

In *Beanpole,* Park introduced her first female **protagonist**. Another novel, *Buddies*, explores the issue of popularity among teenage girls. And, *The Kid in the Red Jacket* features a young female character named Molly Vera Thompson.

Park tackled some important issues in her books, too. *The Graduation of Jake Moon* features a boy whose grandfather has **Alzheimer's disease**. Jake must learn how to deal with his feelings as his grandfather's illness becomes worse.

In 1995, Park's most serious book was published. *Mick Harte Was Here* is about a boy who dies in a bicycle accident. He dies because he was not wearing a helmet. The book features the boy's sister talking about her dead brother. She also talks about how the family deals with the tragedy.

Park wrote *Mick Harte Was Here* after a similar accident happened in her neighborhood. She wanted to use her writing talent to teach kids the importance of wearing a helmet. It took her longer to write *Mick Harte* than any of her other books. She found it hard to find a balance between humor and sadness. *Mick Harte Was Here* remains one of her favorite books.

Park says that her sons had a strong influence on her writing. They kept her tuned in to situations that are humorous to children. But she addressed serious issues, too. **Mick Harte Was Here** *stresses the importance of wearing a bike helmet.*

Junie B. Jones

In 1992, Park introduced a brand-new character. She was a five-year-old bundle of energy named Junie B. Jones. Her first appearance is in *Junie B. Jones and the Stupid, Smelly Bus.* The book tells how Junie B. is afraid to ride home on the bus. She has heard that mean kids will pour chocolate milk in her hair. So, she hides in a supply closet at school.

The Junie B. Jones series is aimed at beginning readers. At first, Park only planned to write four Junie B. books. But, the series is still going strong more than 10 years later. Junie B. has also finally moved on to first grade after nine years in kindergarten!

Even though she has moved up a grade, Junie B. still has some problems with **grammar**. Her speech includes incorrect words like "funner," "fluffery," or "bestest." Some parents have complained about the Junie B. Jones books because of her bad grammar. They also don't like the books because they think Junie B. is too naughty. They say she sets a bad example for children.

However, this criticism does not bother Park. She says many kids have less-than-perfect **grammar**. And, she thinks Junie B.'s mistakes make her more real to readers. Plus, Park does not believe that all books should have heavy moral lessons. She thinks some stories should just be fun to read.

Park based the character of Junie B. on Molly Vera Thompson from **The Kid in the Red Jacket.**

Forever Five

On average, Park writes two Junie B. Jones books a year. Each book takes her several months to create. She wrote her first book on a **portable** typewriter. Now she uses a computer. If she has a **deadline**, she works until she meets it.

Park usually begins her books with a vague plot idea. Sometimes an idea comes to her in the middle of the night. Other times her husband, her editor, and even her sons help with ideas. Then, she imagines interesting characters to move the story along and make it fun. Sometimes, even Park is surprised at what her characters do and say.

Park jokes that her life is pretty boring. She and her husband and two dogs now live near Phoenix, Arizona. Their two sons are grown and live on their own. Park admits that she likes to take naps and eat frozen M&M's when she's not working. She and her husband also enjoy hiking in the desert.

Park credits her success to one thing. She never completely grew up! She believes childhood is not something to get over like an illness. Park says if people are lucky, they never forget what it is like to be a kid. Even now, Park has no trouble thinking like a five-year-old. And, she says her family will agree.

There has been a lot of interest in making a movie about Junie B. Jones. But Park always says no. She believes the best place for Junie B. to live is in people's imaginations.

Glossary

Alzheimer's disease - an illness that causes forgetfulness, confusion, and overall mental disintegration.

audience - a group of readers, listeners, or spectators.

Children's Choice Award - an award given to a children's author. Winners are chosen by children and young adults.

deadline - a set time before something has to be finished.

dedicate - to commit to a goal or way of life.

genre - a category of art, music, or literature.

grammar - a system of rules that determines the correct way to speak, write, and use language.

manuscript - a book or article written by hand or typed before being published.

narrate - to tell a story. A person who narrates is a narrator.

portable - able to be carried or moved.

protagonist - the main character of a story.

real estate - property, which includes buildings and land.

unique - being the only one of its kind.

Web Sites

To learn more about Barbara Park, visit ABDO Publishing Company on the World Wide Web at **www.abdopublishing.com**. Web sites about Park are featured on our Book Links page. These links are routinely monitored and updated to provide the most current information available.

Park wrote a three-book series called The Geek Chronicles. This series is about three geeky friends who don't let their lack of popularity stop them from having fun and making readers laugh!

Index

ML   10/06